EDGE BOOKS™

THE KIDS' GUIDE TO
LOST CITIES

By Sean Stewart Price

Consultant:
Dr. Timothy L. McAndrews,
Director of Archaeological Studies
University of Wisconsin-La Crosse

CAPSTONE PRESS
a capstone imprint

Edge Books are published by Capstone Press,
151 Good Counsel Drive, P.O. Box 669, Mankato, Minnesota 56002.
www.capstonepub.com

 Books published by Capstone Press are manufactured with paper
containing at least 10 percent post-consumer waste.

Library of Congress Cataloging-in-Publication Data
Price, Sean Stewart.
 The kids' guide to lost cities / by Sean Stewart Price.
 p. cm. — (Edge. Kids' guides)
 Summary: "Describes various lost cities, what caused their downfalls, and how
they were discovered"—Provided by publisher.
 Includes bibliographical references and index.
 ISBN 978-1-4296-6009-9 (library binding)
 1. Extinct cities—Juvenile literature. 2. Cities and towns, Ancient—Juvenile
literature. 3. Civilization, Ancient—Juvenile literature. I. Title. II. Series.
CC176.P75 2012
930.1—dc22   2011002488

Editorial Credits
Mandy Robbins, editor; Matt Bruning and Juliette Peters, designers;
 Wanda Winch, media researcher; Eric Manske, production specialist

Photo Credits
Akg-images: Peter Connolly, 24; Alamy: Ace Stock Limited, 12, Image of Africa
Photobank/Nick Greaves, 22, The Print Collector, 7; Capstone, 9 (top); Corbis:
roger Ressmeyer, 10; Getty Images Inc.: Hulton Archive, 14; John F. Kennedy
Library, 27; Landov: dpa/Horst Pfeiffer, 15 (middle); Mary Evans Picture
Library: Illustrated London News Ltd., 26; Shutterstock: Alex Staroseltsev,
cover, 1 (compass), Amy Nichole Harris, 16-17, arazu, cover (top), 4, beboy,
11, casinozack, 3, 7 (temple background), Eastimages, 25, EpicStockMedia, 9
(bottom), gary yim, 5, Hannah Gleghorn, 3 (Aztec calendar design), Hibrida,
23, Irina_QQQ, grunge flower design, Jakub Gruchot, 20, Jarno Gonzalez
Zarraonandia, cover (bottom), Javarman, parchment design, mary 416, 13,
MaxFX, 8, Molodec, cover, 1 (scroll), OPIS, 21, PILart, earth vector design,
Zeljko Radojko, 15 (bottom); SuperStock Inc: The Art Archives, 6, F1 Online,
18-19; William K. Hartmann: Planetary Science Institute, 28-29

Printed in the United States of America in Stevens Point, Wisconsin.
032011   006111WZF11

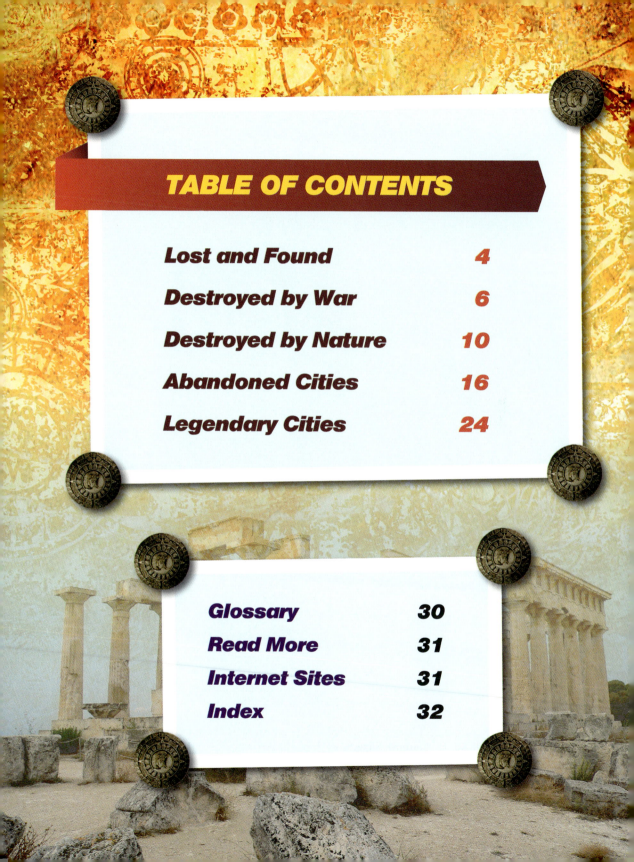

TABLE OF CONTENTS

LOST AND FOUND

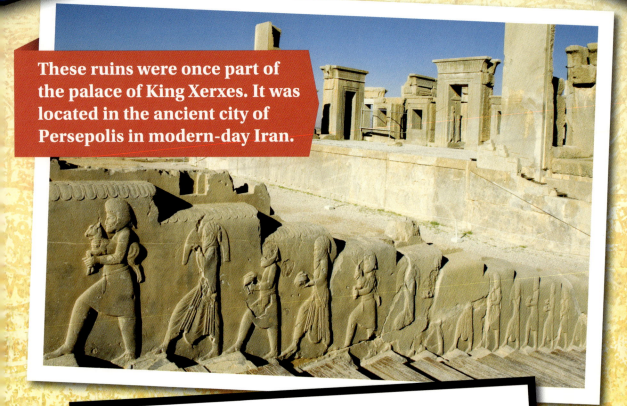

These ruins were once part of the palace of King Xerxes. It was located in the ancient city of Persepolis in modern-day Iran.

How does an entire city become "lost?" Sometimes a city is destroyed, and its location is forgotten. Some cities are abandoned. And other cities are lost because they were never really there. They are cities of legends that many people wrongly believe existed.

Pyramids are a common feature in many ancient ruins.

Lost cities have been rediscovered on every continent. And each one is like a time machine. It can remind people of the way things were long ago. Some lost cities have been found by adventurers. But today **archaeologists** do most of the searching. It can take years for scientists to slowly uncover a lost city. Once it's uncovered, examining a city can tell us many things. It can shed light on old legends. It can show us how ancient people lived. And it can show us mistakes people made that caused their city to fail.

archaeologist—a scientist who studies how people lived in the past

5

DESTROYED BY WAR

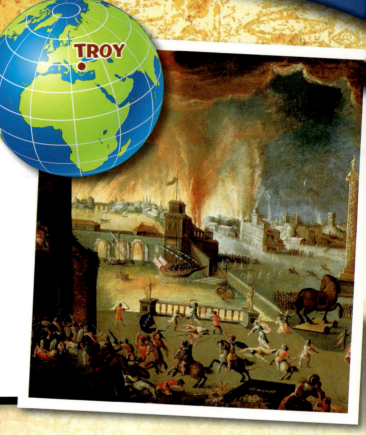

TROY

The ancient Greek poet Homer wrote *The Iliad* and *The Odyssey*. These poems describe a city called Troy. They also describe a war fought between the Trojans and the Greeks. In the end, Troy was captured and burned.

By the late 1800s, many people assumed that the story of Troy was a legend. But Heinrich Schliemann was sure Troy existed. After studying Homer's works, he believed Troy lay buried on a hilltop in modern-day western Turkey. The rivers, ocean shoreline, and mountains all lined up the way the poems described them.

Schliemann began digging. He shocked the world by discovering several cities built one on top of another. Most scholars believe that Troy is probably the city archaeologists call Troy VII-a.

Troy VII-a existed during the time period when Homer's poems were written. It was also destroyed by fire.

Heinrich Schliemann was a wealthy German businessman.

Some people still believe Troy might be somewhere else. But most think that one of the cities at Schliemann's mound is probably the real Troy.

Ruins at Troy VII-a give clues as to what life may have been like for the Trojans.

Today Heinrich Schliemann gets most of the credit for discovering Troy. But other people guessed correctly at its location before him. Twenty years before Schliemann, a man named Frank Calvert began digging at the same site. He came up with some evidence of a city. But he did not have the money to keep digging. Before Calvert, Scottish journalist Charles Maclaren guessed the correct location of the site. But he never went there to prove it.

Troy and Popular Culture

Even before Troy was rediscovered, Homer's poems had a huge effect on popular culture. *The Iliad* and *The Odyssey* have inspired thousands of other writers. They include William Shakespeare and the poet Byron. But they also include modern writers such as Rick Riordan. He wrote the book series Percy Jackson and the Olympians.

Fun Fact:

Dozens of high school and college sports teams are called "Trojans."

POMPEII

About 2,000 years ago, Pompeii was a lovely seaside resort. It sat in the shadow of Mount Vesuvius. The mountain's sloping sides were perfect for growing grapes and olives. Charming Pompeii became a playground for Rome's wealthiest citizens.

POMPEII

The uncovered remains of Pompeii show that it was once a great city.

But Mount Vesuvius had a secret—it was a volcano. Vesuvius hadn't erupted for more than 1,000 years. That changed in AD 79. Early in the morning on August 24, ash began pouring out of the top of Mount Vesuvius. It dusted the streets and buildings of Pompeii.

Around 1:00 p.m., the volcano erupted. Melted rock and ash shot 19 miles (31 kilometers) into the air and fell on Pompeii. Daylight turned to blackness in minutes.

Within three hours, the streets of Pompeii were covered in 1 foot (0.3 meters) of pebbles and stones. Most of Pompeii's population of 20,000 fled at this time. About 2,000 people chose to stay in the city. They all died. The eruption left Pompeii buried under rock and ash. The city became a distant memory.

Fun Fact:

Rocks the size of a fist came whistling down from Mount Vesuvius and killed people as they fled.

Those who died left body-shaped holes in the ash. Scientists poured plaster into the holes to create plaster models of the volcano's victims.

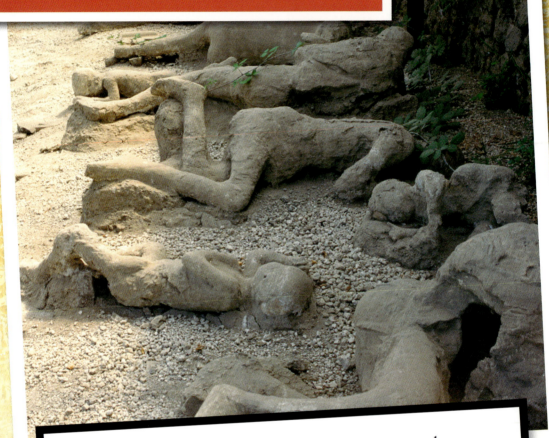

Pompeii and the nearby city of Herculaneum lay buried until the 1700s. Farmers digging wells in the area found ancient vases, jewelry, and other hints of an ancient city. Many people came searching for buried treasure. By the 1800s, scientists had taken over the digging process. Eventually, most of the city was uncovered.

Will It Happen Again?

Archaeologists try to learn from the past to prevent future disasters. Mount Vesuvius has erupted many times since AD 79, most recently in 1944. This relatively minor blast killed 26 people. Today large cities lie close to the volcano. A major eruption would affect more than 600,000 people.

Scientists discovered perfectly preserved tools, dishes, and other everyday objects. They also uncovered detailed **murals** showing activities from Roman life. These findings helped scientists determine what life was like for ancient Romans. In fact, almost everything we know about Roman daily life comes from Pompeii.

mural—a large work of art on a wall or a ceiling

DUNWICH

In the Middle Ages (AD 500 to 1500), the city of Dunwich was one of England's largest ports. But its residents lived in the wrong place. The sea was gradually washing away their city. The water moved inland at a rate of up to 1 yard (0.9 m) per year.

DUNWICH

The ruins of Dunwich Church still stand at the edge of the sea.

Storms made the situation worse. In 1286 a huge storm swept many of the town's buildings into the sea. Two more fierce storms in 1328 and 1347 swept hundreds more houses, churches, and businesses into the sea. Today only a small village is left of Dunwich.

RUNGHOLT

The German city of Rungholt came to an even more dramatic end than Dunwich. Rungholt was an important port city on an island in the North Sea. In 1362 it was hit by a massive storm. The ocean rose, causing many towns to flood.

At least 25,000 people died in areas around the North Sea, including most of the 2,000 people in Rungholt. The storm that hit Rungholt is called the *Grote Mandraenke*. It is German for "a great drowning of men."

Artifacts from flooded cities are found along shorelines and on the muddy ocean floor.

Fun Fact:

Both Dunwich and Rungholt have the same creepy legend. It says that on stormy nights you can hear the bells of the sunken churches coming from the sea.

ABANDONED CITIES

MACHU PICCHU

In 1911 Hiram Bingham heard about a lost city in the mountains of Peru. He set out to find it. Bingham met local farmers who knew about the city. They guided him through jungles and up high cliffs. Finally, the steep ground leveled out. Bingham gazed in wonder at the stone walls of a once-great city.

The Incas built Machu Picchu around AD 1450. Researchers believe the city was built, occupied, and abandoned all within 100 years.

The Incan empire was under attack in the 1500s. The Spanish invaded present-day Peru looking for gold and silver. They destroyed other Inca cities. But it didn't seem possible that the Spanish would have found Machu Picchu so high up in the mountains.

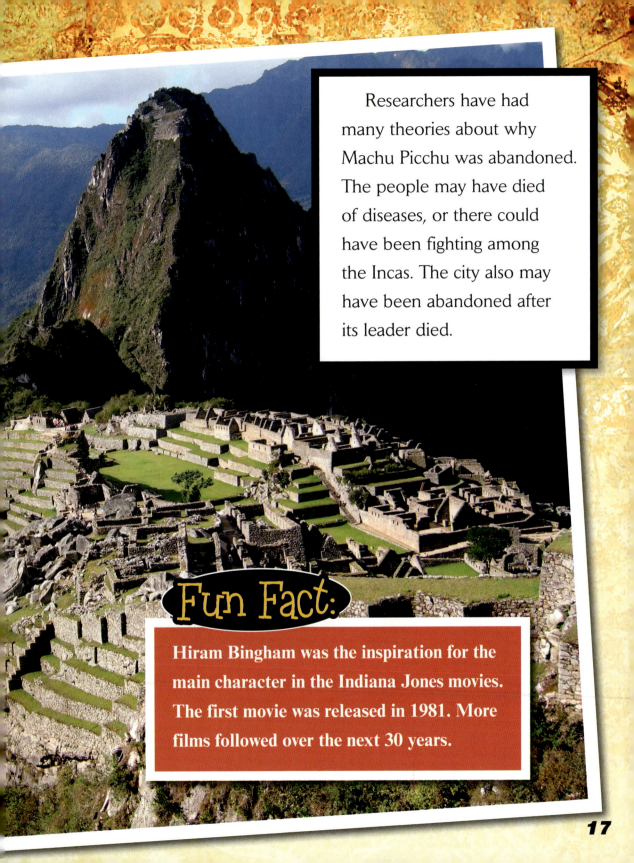

Researchers have had many theories about why Machu Picchu was abandoned. The people may have died of diseases, or there could have been fighting among the Incas. The city also may have been abandoned after its leader died.

Fun Fact:

Hiram Bingham was the inspiration for the main character in the Indiana Jones movies. The first movie was released in 1981. More films followed over the next 30 years.

ANGKOR

ANGKOR

From the 800s to the 1400s, Angkor served as the capital of the Khmer empire. This area is now part of Cambodia. At the city's peak, Angkor was home to at least 500,000 people.

Historians disagree as to why Angkor collapsed. A change in the official religion from **Hinduism** to **Buddhism** caused a lot of problems between citizens. Invasions by neighboring people also weakened the empire. Poor environmental planning played a role as well. The Khmer government tore down surrounding jungle to create farmland. But over-farming caused the soil to go bad. Growing food became very difficult.

Hinduism—a religion practiced mainly in India; Hindus promote harmony and believe that various gods are different forms of the Supreme Deity

Buddhism—a religion based on the teachings of Buddha that is practiced mainly in eastern and central Asia

By the mid-1400s, Angkor was abandoned. Its great temples became overgrown jungle. Europeans visited these ruins from time to time. In 1860 Frenchman Henri Mouhot wrote about Angkor. His drawings and descriptions captured people's imaginations. The city became a popular tourist destination.

Fun Fact:

Angkor is famous for its detailed carvings. Most notable are giant carvings of human heads.

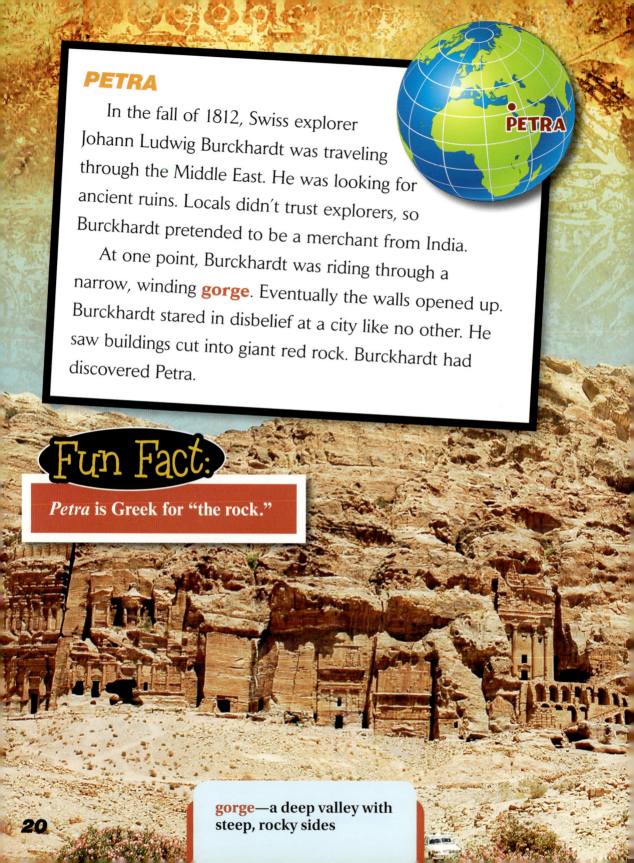

PETRA

In the fall of 1812, Swiss explorer Johann Ludwig Burckhardt was traveling through the Middle East. He was looking for ancient ruins. Locals didn't trust explorers, so Burckhardt pretended to be a merchant from India.

At one point, Burckhardt was riding through a narrow, winding **gorge**. Eventually the walls opened up. Burckhardt stared in disbelief at a city like no other. He saw buildings cut into giant red rock. Burckhardt had discovered Petra.

Fun Fact:

Petra is Greek for "the rock."

gorge—a deep valley with steep, rocky sides

Who Built Petra?

The Nabateans built Petra around 100 BC. They were traders. Their city protected key trading routes in the Middle East. But the trading routes changed over time, and many people left Petra. Earthquakes in AD 363 and 551 probably forced the rest of the people to leave.

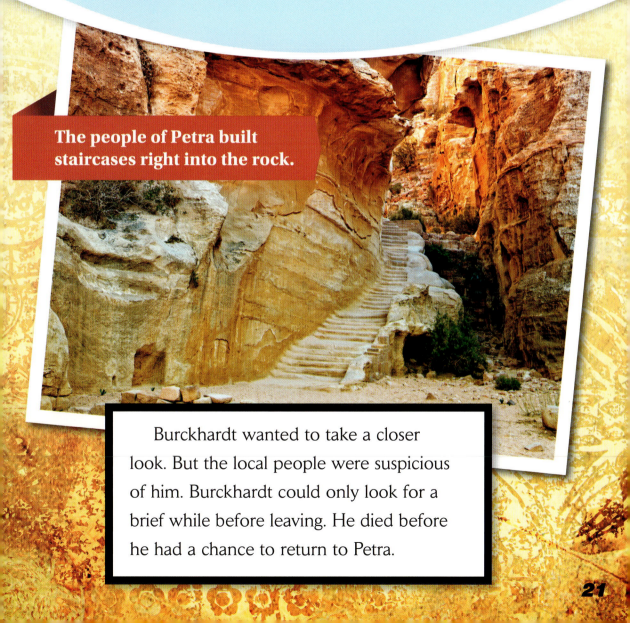

The people of Petra built staircases right into the rock.

Burckhardt wanted to take a closer look. But the local people were suspicious of him. Burckhardt could only look for a brief while before leaving. He died before he had a chance to return to Petra.

GREAT ZIMBABWE

On September 5, 1871, German adventurer Karl Mauch came upon an abandoned city in southern Africa. He had found the city of Great Zimbabwe. The city had tall stone walls and towers that reached even higher. These were the largest ruins in Africa.

GREAT ZIMBABWE

The stone walls of Great Zimbabwe protected the people from enemies and wild animals.

Mauch didn't think Africans could have built this amazing city. In the 1800s, Europeans thought African people were uncivilized. Mauch thought Great Zimbabwe must have been built by the Queen of Sheeba, a queen mentioned in the Bible.

By the 1930s, archaeologist Gertrude Caton-Thompson had proven Mauch wrong. She studied the ruins and artifacts. She also spoke with local people. Her findings showed that Africans had indeed built Great Zimbabwe around AD 1100.

African Continent

Zimbabwe

Great Zimbabwe reached its peak around 1300, but it was abandoned by 1700. Why? That remains a mystery. It was originally a key trading hub. Perhaps trade routes shifted, causing the people to leave.

Fun Fact:

The country of Zimbabwe is named for Great Zimbabwe.

LEGENDARY CITIES

ATLANTIS

About 2,400 years ago, Greek **philosopher** Plato retold stories he had heard about an island in the Atlantic Ocean. He called the island Atlantis. The island was said to be hit by earthquakes and floods. According to Plato, Atlantis disappeared in "a single dreadful day and night." Since Plato's time, hundreds of writers have guessed about where Atlantis was and what it was like. Yet there is very little evidence that Atlantis ever existed.

Many people imagine Atlantis was a city surrounded by water.

philosopher—a person who studies truth, wisdom, knowledge, and the nature of reality

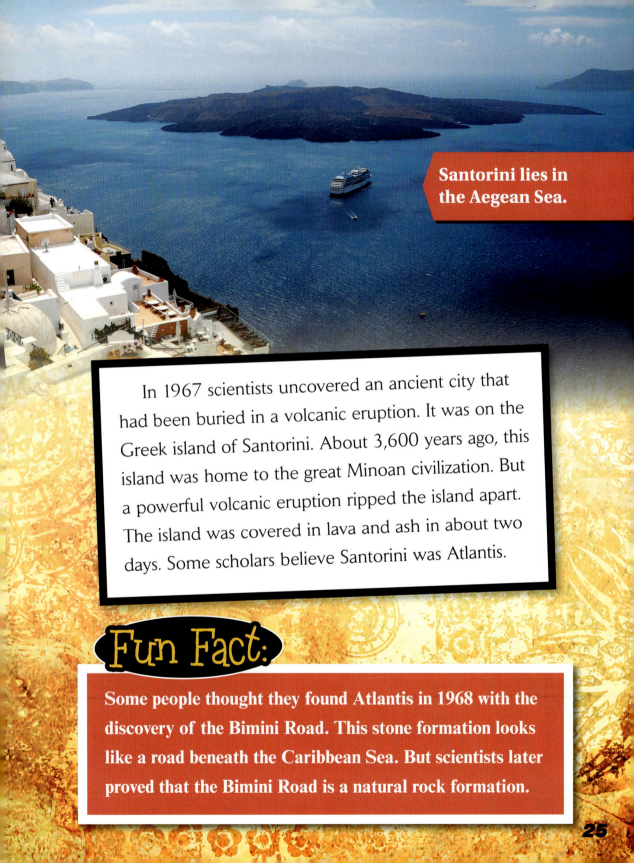

In 1967 scientists uncovered an ancient city that had been buried in a volcanic eruption. It was on the Greek island of Santorini. About 3,600 years ago, this island was home to the great Minoan civilization. But a powerful volcanic eruption ripped the island apart. The island was covered in lava and ash in about two days. Some scholars believe Santorini was Atlantis.

Fun Fact:

Some people thought they found Atlantis in 1968 with the discovery of the Bimini Road. This stone formation looks like a road beneath the Caribbean Sea. But scientists later proved that the Bimini Road is a natural rock formation.

Many people imagine that Camelot was the ideal English Kingdom.

CAMELOT

According to **folktales**, King Arthur was a wise English king during the Middle Ages. Arthur surrounded himself with brave knights like Sir Lancelot and Sir Percival. Arthur and his "Knights of the Round Table" lived in the famous castle of Camelot.

folktale—a legend handed down by word of mouth

Perfection

Camelot has come to mean a "perfect place at a perfect time." President John F. Kennedy's widow, Jacqueline, described her husband's short term in office as a type of Camelot. Many people use the term to describe Kennedy's years in office.

Many historians doubt that Camelot or Arthur ever existed. But others have spent a lot of time chasing the legend of Camelot. If there ever was a King Arthur, he probably lived in western England. But there are many possible sites in that area. One of them is called Cadbury Castle, although it is not really a castle. In the 1960s, scientists found that the mound had served as a **fortress** in the 500s.

fortress—a place that has been strengthened against military attack

CIBOLA

In 1539 a Spanish priest named Marcos de Niza reported an amazing find in present-day New Mexico. He claimed to have seen the legendary golden city of Cibola. Spanish explorers had heard stories from American Indians about cities made of gold.

Francisco Coronado led Spain's search for Cibola. But the city he found was not made of gold.

Two years later, the Spanish sent out a team of explorers to search for Cibola. But the golden city was not where de Niza had said it was. Instead the explorers found only a village of mud buildings. Had de Niza lied, or had he not remembered the correct location?

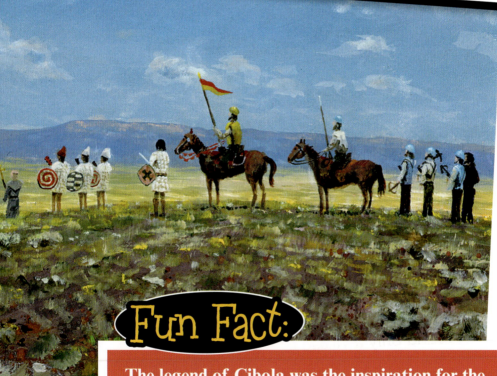

Most people believe that if Cibola existed it would have been found by now. But discoveries of other lost cities have shown that it pays to be open-minded. Are there more cities that lie buried, just waiting to be uncovered? Perhaps they are right beneath our feet!

Fun Fact:

The legend of Cibola was the inspiration for the hit movie *National Treasure: Book of Secrets*.

archaeologist (ar-kee-AH-luh-jist)—a scientist who studies how people lived in the past

Buddhism (BOO-diz-uhm)—a religion based on the teachings of Buddha that is practiced mainly in eastern and central Asia

folktale (FOHK-tayl)—a legend handed down by word of mouth

fortress (FOR-triss)—a place that has been strengthened against a military attack

gorge (GORJ)—a deep valley with steep, rocky sides

Hinduism (HIN-doo-iz-uhm)—a religious philosophy practiced mainly in India; Hindus believe that they act in harmony with universal laws and that various gods are different forms of the Supreme Deity

mural (MYU-ruhl)—a large work of art on a wall or a ceiling

philosopher (fuh-LOSS-uh-fur)—a person who studies truth, wisdom, knowledge, and the nature of reality

port (PORT)—a harbor or place where boats and ships can dock or anchor safely

Read More

De Winter, James. *Discovering Lost Cities and Pirate Gold.* Extreme Adventures! Mankato, Minn.: Capstone Press, 2010.

Linneìa, Sharon. *Mysteries Unwrapped.* Lost Civilizations. New York: Sterling Pub. Co., 2009.

Walker, Kathryn. *The Mystery of Atlantis.* Unsolved! New York: Crabtree Pub. Co., 2010.

Internet Sites

FactHound offers a safe, fun way to find Internet sites related to this book. All of the sites on FactHound have been researched by our staff.

Here's all you do:

Visit *www.facthound.com*

Type in this code: 9781429660099

Super-cool stuff!

INDEX